valérie weill & philippe chancel

london in store

preface by hattie ellis

Thames & Hudson

First published in the United Kingdom in 2005 by
Thames & Hudson Ltd, 181A High Holborn, London WC1V 7QX

www.thamesandhudson.com

British Library Cataloguing-in-Publication Data
A catalogue record for this book is available from
the British Library

ISBN-13: 978-0-500-51255-5
ISBN-10: 0-500-51255-8

Printed and bound in China by Midas Printing

preface

by hattie ellis

Retail bombards us with so many images, beckoning us to come, to touch, to spend, that we shrug off most of them. In doing so, we inadvertently blank out a large part of our everyday surroundings. With their remarkable books, Valérie Weill and Philippe Chancel make us stop and look again, through the alternative windows of their photographs, to discover what else can be found in shops. This is not necessarily what the proprietors wish to sell, or what we want to buy.

Commerce is materialistic, but these pictures are full of humanity. Few people appear in them yet they are all the more present in their absence. They are there in the poignant shelves of filed lives in the monumental masons (page 29); in the intimate heat of Gary Hyde's heel, pinned to the wall, along with his invoice, in a thermal image at the shoemaker's (page 99); and in the used shoes that have walked away from past owners and await new dancing partners in the vintage clothing emporium (page 213). Disorderly schoolboys will soon fill the flying ghosts of uniforms (pages 65 and 93), customers will dial up mature Katrina, Leggy English Blonde (page 63), and it is her hands that will supply a luxurious massage, a minute from Marble Arch.

The owners are shown by their business cards rather than their faces, and this, too, starts to summon up characters in our minds. We seek their personalities in the design of their shops, some of which are laid out with the precision and verve of graphic art. Just as front pages of newsprint are designed daily by sub-editors to catch their readers' sliding eyes (page 19), every trader knows you can move an unnoticed object ten centimetres and hit a hot spot for a sale. The shop display offers an opportunity for individual style and humour. Someone thought of sweeping up bags of penne into cresting waves of pasta in the Italian restaurant (page 105), and someone at Oops (page 47) placed the rubber mask of Saddam Hussein alongside Tony Blair and the two George Bushes.

But the main focus of the book is the overlooked rather than the obvious, and in this way Weill and Chancel subvert these shop displays. The up-market auction house looks cheap (page 79). James Smith & Sons, one of the most beautiful shops in London, is shown not by its outstanding Victorian frontage but by a jumble of cane umbrella handles and a grey plastic till (page 161). In contrast, an ordinary café's condiment bottles form a tabletop Manhattan skyline (page 51), and there is a gaudy glory in the world of fudge and jelly beans (page 95). Whilst some of the displays are charmingly old-fashioned, like the cake stands of children's shoes (page 143), and others – although few – are intentionally beautiful (LASSCO's montage of old objects on page 145), most are more oddly attractive. Multi-coloured tower blocks of crisp boxes are almost glamorous once they fill a page (page 35), and sexy sports cars look like a cross between bananas and ski-boots (page 21). The strangeness of these shops, when looking at them out of context like this, reveals something new about the places and the things that they sell, and so we see both afresh.

There is a retail saying that 'the single bloom is left alone; the bank of flowers sells'. Weill and Chancel's vision makes numbers work to another effect. It is strange to see the chorus line of corpses and piles of hooves in the butcher's (page 23), the dry-stone wall of suits (page 25), the death knells of health warnings on the cigarette packets (page 37), the flamingo flock of hairdryers (page 57) or the army of boots (page 67). The bank of wall-fixtures (page 17) becomes an abstract design of geometric shapes, not merely switches, sockets and plugs.

Whilst some of the shops are cluttered, others are sparse. This may be intentional, highlighting the exclusivity of the chocolates (page 129), or cultural, such as in the noodle bar and Japanese restaurant (pages 39 and 89), or accidental. The pair of orchids left in the florists (page 203) creates an aura of sadness about the space. Weill and Chancel's approach is all the more effective because they shoot as they find, walking around the city allowing themselves to be surprised by what they encounter, rather than placing the objects for their purposes. These found still lifes have been positioned only by their observations.

With them, we enter new worlds through their unfamiliar props, such as 100 per cent kanekalon hair extensions (page 71), or the 'air-brushed' texture of wigs (page 137). Some of the pictures shake us out of the familiar by verging on the surreal or pointing up the incongruous. There is a room of fireplaces (page 33), a room within a room (page 121) and the toy room, its scale ambiguous – it could be tiny or huge (page 27). We see caged hats (page 41), headless polo players (page 55), Liberty's folded fields of flowers (page 135) and a fake dead tiger with saucepans on its back in a shop called Pure Life (page 97). And what are those ovoids at Sketch (page 59)? If many of the images reveal the unusual or the unseen in the familiar, part of the book's seam of irony also makes the most unusual places look relatively normal, such as the stuffed animals at the taxidermist (page 75).

There are more sly glances, too, for example at the old pub where plastic wrapping hangs off its new 'heritage' displays (page 31). Small details within the pictures tell stories. The old-fashioned barbers has, if you look carefully, a small HIV/Aids sign (page 141). When once the proprietor of such a spare masculine world, with its straight chrome and gleaming black, might have suggested to his customers 'something for the weekend', now he offers health promotion. The level of observation in the photography makes you look further into the pictures and draw wider connections. The clocks shaped like countries in Elsi's in Brixton (page 45) includes war-torn Somalia, its time muffled by small pieces of foam on its hands.

This is a route through London that encompasses both mass-production and the hand-crafted temples of the elite. Some of these shops are outstanding collections, gathered in by owners who are akin to curators, such is their depth of knowledge. From my own explorations of London's shops, I know that Nicholas Walt, the proprietor of artists' materials merchants L. Cornelissen & Son (page 187), has a collection of historic hues stashed in his basement, including a rare jarful of the legendary Indian Yellow. This extraordinarily beautiful colour was made by feeding cattle with mango leaves and collecting and concentrating the earth splattered with their urine. The pigment was banned in the nineteenth century because of the cruelty involved in feeding the animals an unnatural diet. You can spot the pigment in Indian miniatures; it is exactly the rich gold of a perfectly ripe mango.

The customers of interesting shops are as unusual as their owners, goods and suppliers. James Smith's, the umbrella and stick experts (page 161), attracts the sort of eccentric who still carries a parasol or a tightly furled black brolly in the crook of one arm. The assistants never know who will step through the door – American tourists, an old lady off to study orangutans in Borneo, an African chief seeking a tribal stick or a man in a cloak inquiring if Jesus Christ has been in today. By loitering a little in such places you soon come across characters like these.

And so this road of images through a city of commerce allows us to be consumers of life. It makes us see shops as places where you can notice the telling detail and encounter happenstance, just as Weill and Chancel do. After browsing these pages, there is one immediate response: to seek out places you might not usually enter, or to reconsider others you frequent, and to walk in with no other purpose other than to look. By so doing, you are rebelling against the functionality of being a spending unit in a selling emporium, instead you become a curious non-shopper on the front-line against mere consumerism. Whatever your reasons, you are no longer a radio dial whirling too fast to pick up the frequency of what is interesting in everyday surroundings. By looking through display, by rejecting the hurry and grab of the get and the spend, you walk away from the brightly bland anonymity of modern retail and get back in step with the real life of the street.

the stores

Presented By

LORDS
Builders & Decorators
Merchants

119/121 Westbourne Grove
London W2 4UP

Tel: 020 7221 4756
      020 7313 7480(Paints)
Fax: 020 7792 9513
E-mail: info@lordsdiy.com

www.lordsbuildersmerchants.com

Pread Street
Tel 0171 4023117

Lamborghini London

Dominic Lancaster
General Manager

Lamborghini London
Melton Court
27 Old Brompton Road
London SW7 3TD
Tel 020 7589 1472
Fax 020 7589 1593
Mobile 07730 927 928
sales@lamborghini.co.uk

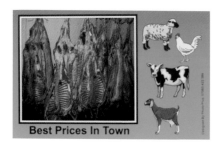

HUNTSMAN

--- SAVILE ROW, LONDON ---

Peter Smith
Sales Director

11 SAVILE ROW, LONDON W1S 3PS
telephone 020 7734 7441 *facsimile* 020 7287 2937
email mail@h-huntsman.com *web* www.h-huntsman.com

ESTABLISHED 1849

A.ELFES LTD
MONUMENTAL MASONS
ESTABLISHED 1894

HEAD OFFICE

17 OSBORN STREET LONDON E1 6TD
TEL 020 7247 0163 & 020 7247 6025
FAX: 020 7375 0526
web: www.memorialgroup.co.uk
Email: enquiries@memorialgroup.co.uk

THE
MEMORIAL GROUP

IN THE
INTEREST
OF SAFETY
CUSTOMERS ARE
REQUESTED
NOT TO TOUCH
MEMORIALS

The Green man
144 Essex road
Islington N1

020718
0207 226 2692

12

32

ZACO MINI MARKET
175 UPPER STREET
ISLINGTON, LONDON N1 1RG
TEL/FAX: 020 7354 2690

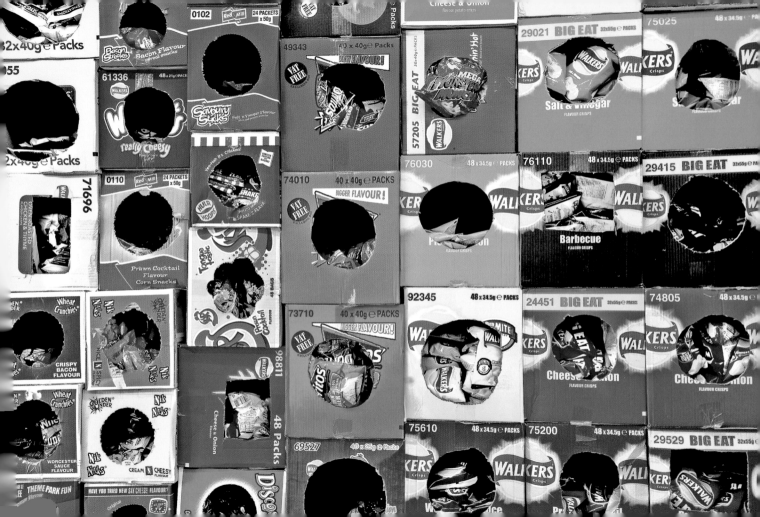

G. Smith and Sons

74 Charing Cross Road
London WC2H 0BG
Tel/Fax: 020 7836 7422

SNUFF BLENDERS AND CIGAR IMPORTERS * SINCE 1869 *

Japanese Restaurant
NAMBU-tei

209A Baker Street,
London NW1 6AB
Tel : 020-7486-5026
Fax: 020-7224-1741

Lunch 12.00 - 3.00 pm (Mon - Fri)
Dinner 6.00 - 11.00 pm (Mon - Sat)

BATES

Gentlemen's Hatter,

21A JERMYN STREET,
ST. JAMES'S LONDON SW1Y 6HP

TELEPHONE/FAX: 020 7734 2722

WWW.BATES-HATS.CO.UK

MODELZONE

Holborn
202 High Holborn
Central London
WC1V 6JS
Tel: (020) 7405 6285
Fax: (020) 7242 1684

stores at
Bluewater
Brighton
Bromley
Crawley
Croydon
Eastbourne
Gateshead
Guildford
Kingston
London
Maidstone
Plymouth
Romford
Sutton

Alag Natarajan

oops
524 Oxford Street
London W1C 1LN

t. +44 (0)20 7629 0810
f. +44 (0)20 7408 1998
e. info@oopsweb.co.uk
www.oopsweb.co.uk

oops™

Telephone:
020-7734 8040

BY APPOINTMENT
TO HER MAJESTY QUEEN ELIZABETH II
GROCERS AND PROVISION MERCHANTS
FORTNUM & MASON PLC LONDON

Facsimile:
020-7437 3278

Fortnum & Mason Plc
181 Piccadilly,
London, WIA 1ER

Presented by ....

A & H BRASS   201-203 Edgware Road   London W2 1ES
Tel: 020 7402 1854   Fax: 020 7402 0110
Email: ahbrass@btinternet.com
Website: www.aandhbrass.co.uk

● Architectural Ironmongery ● Bathroom Accessories ● Light Fittings

RALPH LAUREN

Francis Cronin
SALES ASSOCIATE
FLAGSHIP STORE

No 1 New Bond Street, London W1S 3RL
Tel: 020 7535 4600 Fax: 020 7535 4700
Email: Inbs@poloralphlauren.com

RALPH LAUREN
THE
SUMMER
SALE

Rosa's
Unisex Hairdressing Salon

Open: Tue. to Fri. 9.30am - 6.00pm
Saturday 8.00am - 5.00pm
Closed Monday's

26 Golborne Road, London W10 5PF
Tel: 020-8969 0309

sketch
9 Conduit Street   London W1

Reservations / Enquiries 0870 777 4488

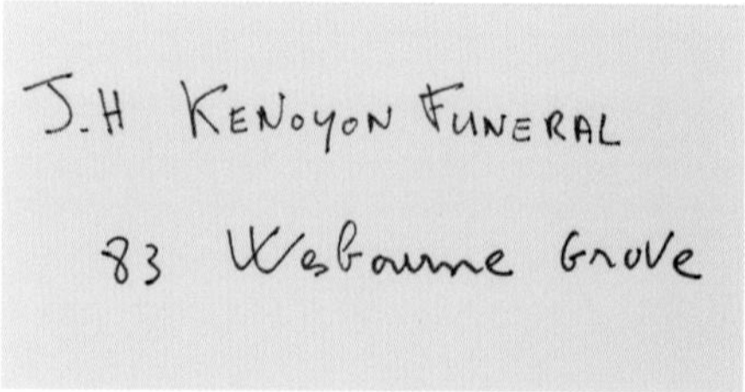

J.H KENOYON FUNERAL

83 Wesbourne Grove

This phone is at

CRIMESTOPPERS
0800 555 111

(020) 7491 3816

JCN DOVER ST O/S 71/72

PICCADILLY

LONDON W1V 9HH

SOS emergency calls -
dial 999 or 112 free
For Police, Ambulance, Fire, Coastguard,
Mountain Rescue, and Cave Rescue

The Samaritans
08457 90 90 90

ChildLine

Message Home Helpline: 0800 700 740

0800 1111

John Lewis

www.johnlewis.com

Oxford Street

300 Oxford Street
London W1A 1EX

Telephone 020 7629 7711
Fax 020 7514 5300
jl_oxford_street@johnlewis.co.uk

HARD WEAR

70 Essex Road, Islington, LONDON N1 8LT
Opening Hours: Mon – Sat 10 am to 6 pm

Tel: 020 7359 8667   Fax: 020 7359 6392
eMail: hard-wear@btconnect.com
web address: www.hard-wear.co.uk

CLOTHING DISCOUNT COMPANY
MENSWEAR

Tel: 020 7242 7116

6 Southampton Row
London WC1B 4AA

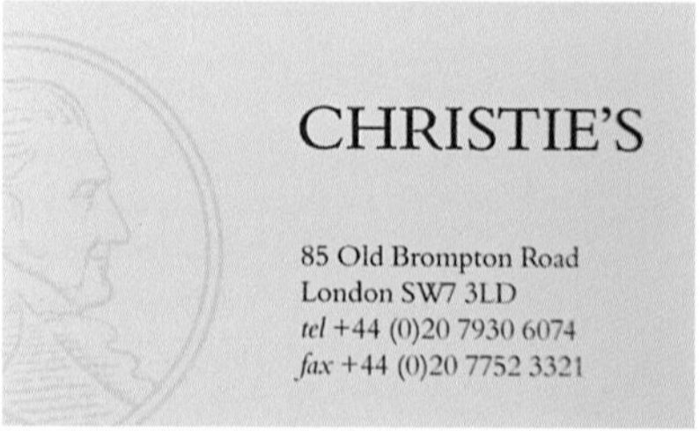

CHRISTIE'S

85 Old Brompton Road
London SW7 3LD
tel +44 (0)20 7930 6074
fax +44 (0)20 7752 3321

SPEEDY NOODLE ®
Good food need not be expensive

506 - 508 Brixton Road,
Brixton, London SW9 8EN

Tel: 020 7326 4888
Fax: 020 7326 0888

Open 7 Days A Week
Monday - Thursday
12noon - 11.30pm
Friday - Sunday
12noon - 1.00am

M·M·E MOTORCYCLE

Spares-Repairs
Sales
Tel/Fax
0207 7296404
Mobile
0796 1365935

20a GRIMSBY STREET
LONDON
E2 6ES

INDEPENDENT CAGIVA MITO SPECIALIST

MARKS &
SPENCER

5 - 7 Liverpool Road
Islington, London N1
Telephone:- 020 7837 2744
www.marksandspencer.com
VAT No: 232 1288 92

Miss T Hughes.
unit 4 old
old spitalfields Market
Brushfield st
London E1 6AA.

PURE LIFE.

350   BETHNAL green

SPECIAL FOOTWEAR
& ORTHOTICS

Anthony Andrews
Master Shoemaker

12 NEW CAVENDISH STREET
LONDON W1G 8UN

TEL **020 7486 4664**   FAX 020 7486 4644
WEBSITE WWW.SPECIALFOOTWEAR.CO.UK
EMAIL INFO@SPECIALFOOTWEAR.CO.UK

FRACTURES

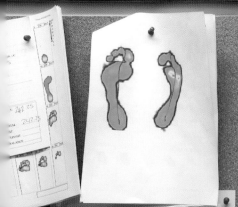

ORTHOTICS

DATE   WANTED BY
NAME
ADDRESS
HOME TEL.   WORK TEL.
NUMBER

DESCRIPTION

NOTES   PRICE
                            TOTAL
                            VAT
                            DEPOSIT
                            BALANCE

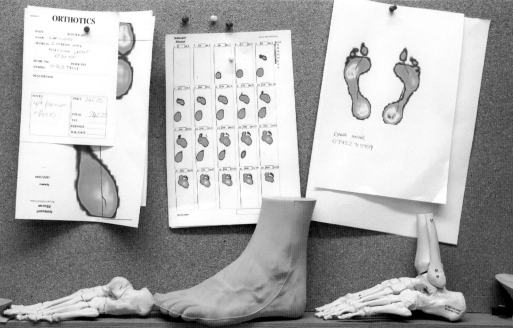

GAIT ANALYSIS

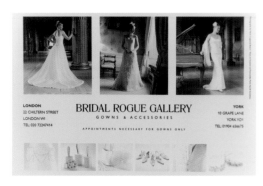

LONDON
22 CHILTERN STREET
LONDON W1
TEL: 020 72247414

BRIDAL ROGUE GALLERY
GOWNS & ACCESSORIES

YORK
10 GRAPE LANE
YORK YO1
TEL: 01904 656675

APPOINTMENTS NECESSARY FOR GOWNS ONLY

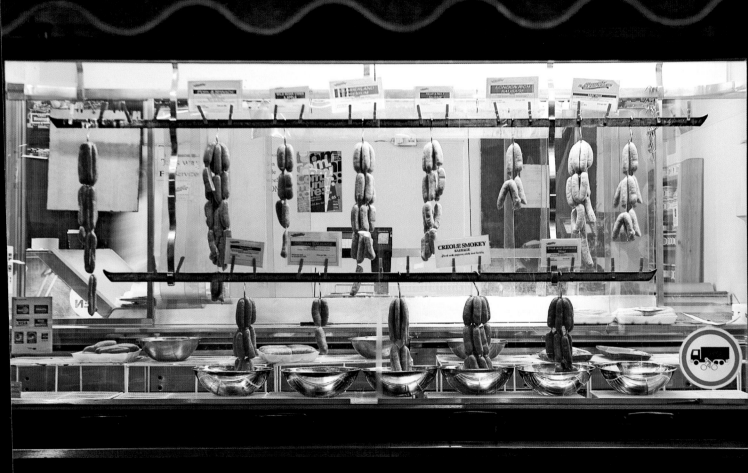

ZIPPI - LONDON
ITALIAN Restaurant
43 WHITE HALL
020 79251249

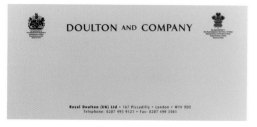

DOULTON AND COMPANY

Royal Doulton (UK) Ltd • 167 Piccadilly • London • W1V 9DE
Telephone: 0207 493 9121 • Fax: 0207 499 3561

£295

£420.00

J Peachy.

146ᴬ DOWNHAM. Rd

SS hight.

[signature]

N 1 near

Sea Food Stall library

119 - 120 Essex Rd

284 Bethnal Green
ROAD LONDON.

S + R kellys Pie e MASH.

Telephone: +44 (0) 20 7734 1420
Facsimile: +44 (0) 20 7734 1721
E-Mail: office@anderson-sheppard.co.uk

Anderson & Sheppard, Ltd.

30, Savile Row, London W1S 3PT

RESTAURANT
LES TROIS GARÇONS

Hassan Michel Stefan

1 CLUB ROW, LONDON. E1 6JX
020 7613 1924
www.lestroisgarcons.com

DOVER STREET MARKET

17-18 Dover Street London W1S 4LT
tel : 020 7518 0680
fax : 020 7518 0681

David Mitchell

PICTURE FRAMES

28 LOAMPIT HILL
LEWISHAM
LONDON SE13 7SL

TEL: 020 8469 0078
FAX: 020 8469 3260
MOBILE: 07958 688290

CLOSED WEDNESDAY & SUNDAY

KARL-LUDWIG REHSE

KARL LUDWIG

COUTURE

2, CHILTERN STREET LONDON W1U 7PR
TEL: 020 7935 6330 FAX: 020 7486 2656

BY APPOINTMENT
TO HER MAJESTY
QUEEN ELIZABETH II
DRESSMAKER

BY APPOINTMENT
TO HM QUEEN ELIZABETH
THE QUEEN MOTHER
DRESSMAKER

Shop 111B, off Commercial Street, Old Spitalfields Market
London E1 6BG ◆ Tel/Fax: 020 7426 0017
E-mail: queenseast1@aol.com

BALLANTYNE
CASHMERE

303 WESTBOURNE GROVE   LONDON W11 2QA
tel +44 (0) 207 792 2563 fax +44 (0) 207 243 5816
www.ballantyne.it

LIBERTY

Liberty plc Regent St. London W1B 5AH
Tel: +44 (0)20 7734 1234
Fax: +44 (0)20 7573 9876

Liberty Print
tana lawn
£17.25

JOHN'S HAIRDRESSING SALON
(GEORGE THOMAS)

223 OLD STREET   0207-253 9232

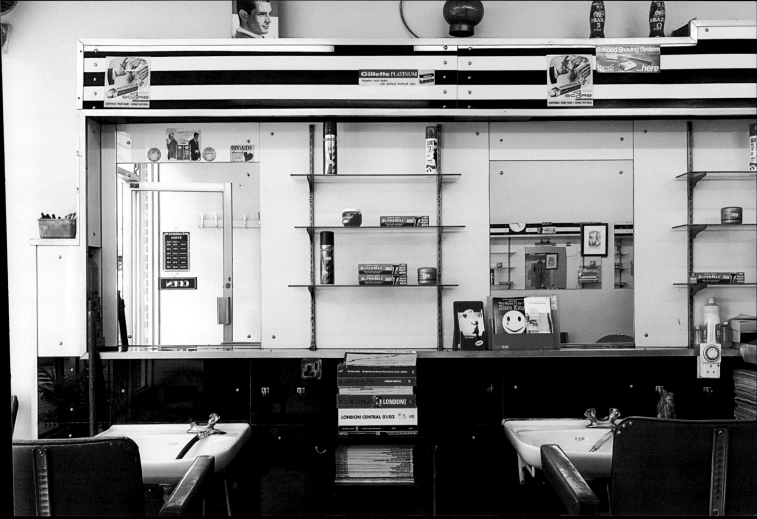

Rachel Riley

Shops :
14 Pont Street, London,
SW1X 9EN, UK.
Tel : 020 7259 5969 Fax : 020 7245 0759

82 Marylebone High Street, London,
W1U 4QW, UK.
Tel : 020 7935 7007 Fax : 020 7935 7004

Workshop in France :
La Roche Froissard, 49350 Gennes,
France. Tel/Fax : 02 41 38 04 93

Mail-order :
Tel : 020 7935 7007 Fax : 020 7935 7004

Email : info@rachelriley.com
Website : www.rachelriley.com

Rachel Riley

LASSCO
ST MICHAEL'S

Ferrous Auger B.A. (Hons) F.A.V.

tel 020 7749 9949
fax 020 7749 9941 *e-mail* ferrous@lassco.co.uk
Mark Street *(off Paul Street)*, London EC2A 4ER

Le MarraKech

Halal Meat Moroccan Food & Craft

Retail & Wholesale

Highly recommended by

the London Food Guide 2000

Mob:07733 004 595

07985 278 751

64 Golborne Road London W10 5PS

Tel:0208 964 8307

PLEASE DO NOT
ASK FOR CREDIT
REFUSAL
OFTEN OFFENDS

EXPERIANCE
HALAL ME

ANGEL CAFE
100 Essex Road N.1.

Tel ....

VAT No: ....

The

AQUATIC
DESIGN CENTRE
Ltd

Aquarium Supplies

107-111 GREAT PORTLAND STREET,
LONDON, W1W 6QG
TEL: 020 7580 6764 FAX: 020 7631 2033
www.aquaticdesign.co.uk

```
          CITY PUBS
     ------------------

FOUNTAINS ABBEY CO736
     109 PRAED ST
      PADDINGTON
        LONDON
      W2   1RL
```

ARTHUR BEALE

YACHT
CHANDLERS

AB
LIMITED

ESTABLISHED
FOUR
CENTURIES

TEL: 020-7836 9034
FAX: 020-7836 5807

194 SHAFTESBURY AVENUE
LONDON · WC2H 8JP

Recyled Computer
Parts and Accessories

No7 Cheshire StreetE2
Off of Brick Lane
0207-613-0069

JAMES SMITH

& SONS (UMBRELLAS) LTD.

———

UMBRELLAS & STICKS

ESTABLISHED 1830

53 NEW OXFORD STREET, WC1A 1BL
Telephone: 020-7836 4731
Fax: 020-7836 4730

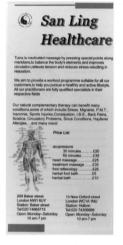

San Ling Healthcare

Tuina is medicated massage by pressing special points along meridians, to balance the body's elements and improves circulation, relieves tension and reduces stress-resulting in relaxation.

We aim to provide a workout programme suitable for all our customers, to help you pursue a healthy and active lifestyle. All our practitioners are fully qualified specialists in their respective fields

Our natural complementary therapy can benefit many conditions, some of which include Stress, Migraine, P.M.T., Insomnia, Sports Injuries, Constipation, I.B.S., Back Pains, Sciatica, Circulatory Problems, Sinus Conditions, Hayfever Allergies....and many more!

Price List

acupressure
       30 minutes.........£20
       60 minutes.........£35
head massage £25
treatment massage £35
foot reflexology £25
herbal foot bath..........£5
herbal bath £10

209 Baker street
London NW1 6UY
Station: Baker street
Tel 020 74968715
Open: Monday–Saturday
    10 am-7 pm

13 New Oxford street
London WC1A 1NU
Station: Holbon
Tel 020 74309889
Open: Monday–Saturday
    10 am-7 pm

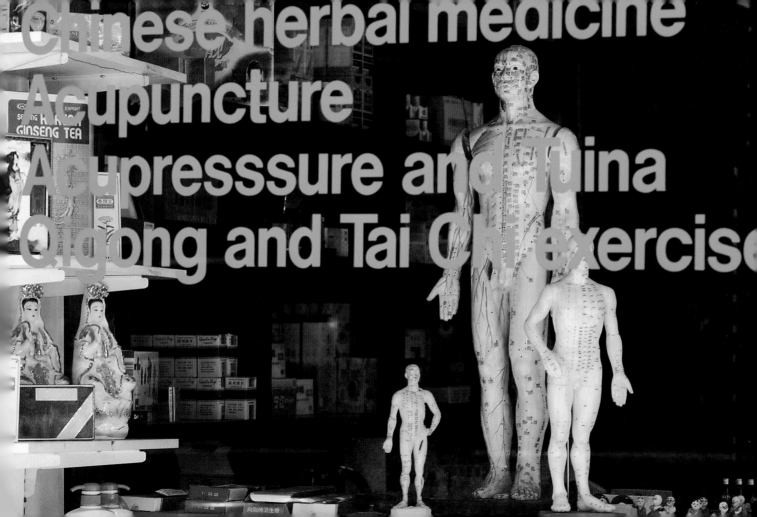

www.waitrose.com
Food shops of the John Lewis Partnership

Doncastle Road, Bracknell Berkshire RG12 8YA
Waitrose Limited Registered Office
171 Victoria Street London SW1E 5NN
VAT No 232 457 280

Waitrose

Urbanism Ltd   January 2004

Old Spitalfields Market Information Sheet

Manager – Eric Graham   Office telephone – 020 7247 8556
                                             Security telephone – 020 377 2883
Welcome to the Old Spitalfields Market.

The Market is currently open everyday except Saturdays with vehicular access for
deliveries only as follows:-

Monday to Friday	0700 hours until 1100 hours
	1500 hours until 1900 hours
Sunday	0700 hours until 0930 hours
	1700 hours until 1900 hours

There is no onsite parking.

Stall Fees
~~THURSDAY ANTIQUES~~   MARKET ONLY   £25
Monday to Friday   £10
Sunday   £65 (subject to availability)

BanglaCity

Continental Supermarket

86 BrickLane, London E1 6RL
Tel : 0207 456 1000
Fax : 0207 655 44 55
E-mail : kalam@banglacity.co.uk

CONTACT DETAILS :

DIRECTOR
MR ABDUL KALAM

0207 456 1000
07714295705

72 Charing Cross Road, London WC2H 0BE. England
Telephone +44 (0)20 7240 1559   Facsimile +44 (0)20 7379 7678
E-mail: gcowan@artbook.co.uk   Website: www.artbook.co.uk

Duplicate Receipt

HARMONY
4 Walkers Court
SOHO London

Harrods Ltd, Knightsbridge, London SW1X 7XL

LOUNGELOVER

1 WHITBY STREET, LONDON E1
020 7012 1234/5
www.loungelover.co.uk

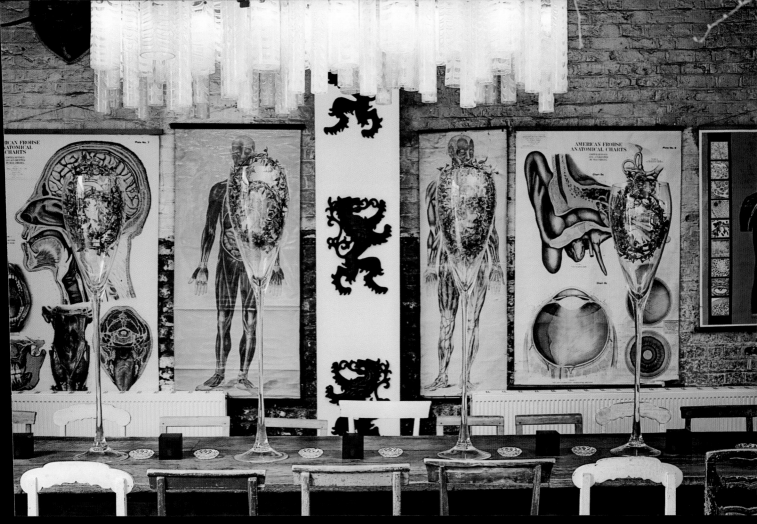

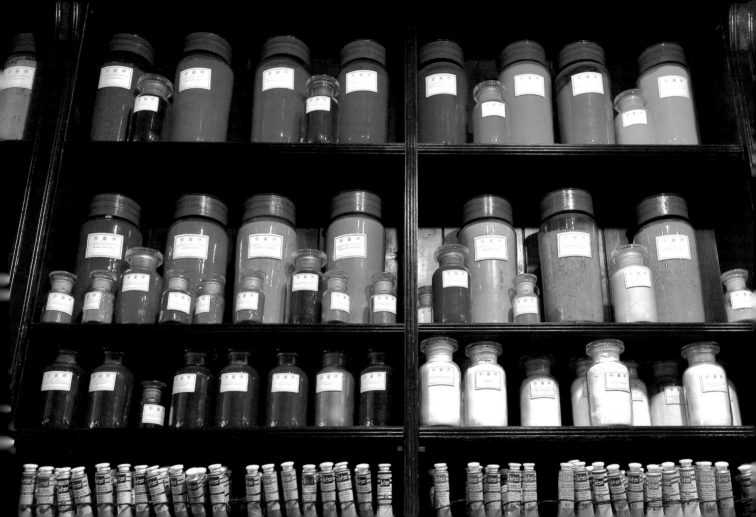

SERVICE WASH NO 05031	WASH		
	SOAP		
THE LAUNDERETTE	EXTRACT		
52 GOLBORNE ROAD	DRY (Number)		
LONDON W10 5PR	SERVICE CHARGE		
	TOTAL		

THE BACK SHOP

Cares for your back

Zahid Malik
Sales and Operations Director

14 New Cavendish Street
London W1G 8UW

Tel: 020 7935 9120/9148
Cell: 079 7061 7320 - Fax: 020 7224 1903
Email: info@thebackshop.co.uk
Web: www.thebackshop.co.uk

INFOMARK LIMITED
GROUND FLOOR
70 OLD BROMPTON ROAD
LONDON SW7 3LQ
TEL: 071-225 1757
VAT No: 645 5214 44

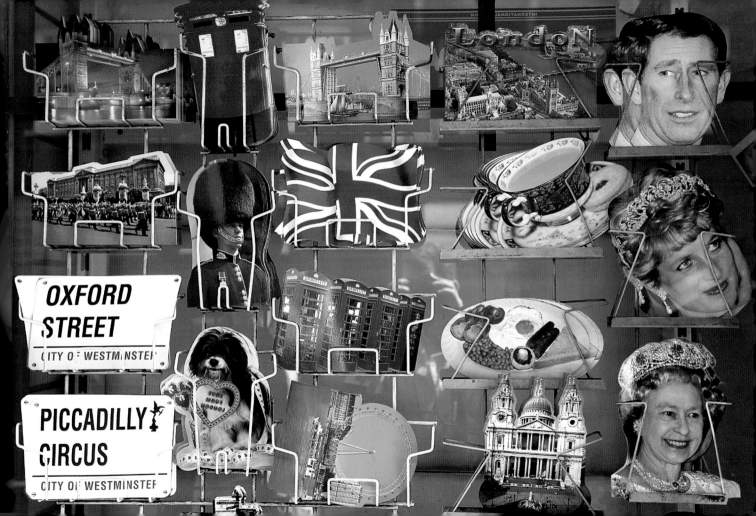

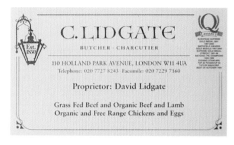

C.LIDGATE

BUTCHER · CHARCUTIER

110 HOLLAND PARK AVENUE, LONDON W11 4UA
Telephone: 020 7727 8243 · Facsimile: 020 7229 7160

Proprietor: David Lidgate

Grass Fed Beef and Organic Beef and Lamb
Organic and Free Range Chickens and Eggs

BUY BEST
188 PORTOBELLO ROAD
LONDON
W11

(0207) 2218876

TIMPSON LIMITED
30/32 KINGSWAY
HOLBORN
LONDON
WC2B 6SD

WITH COMPLIMENTS

117 MOUNT STREET, MAYFAIR, LONDON, W1Y 6HX
TELEPHONE: 0171-499 5831 FACSIMILE: 0171-409 7112

The restaurant will be closed for refurbishment from 19 April – 9 May, and 28 June – 13 September; the café remains open throughout.
In fine weather there is an open-air courtyard café.
Call 020 7300 5608 for further details.

Royal Academy e-mail news
To receive monthly e-mail bulletins with special offers and news on future exhibitions and events, visit royalacademy.org.uk/news

Situated in the heart of the West End between Green Park and Piccadilly Circus.
Buses 9, 14, 19, 22 and 38 stop outside

Jewels by Count Alexander

Royal Crown Jeweller Count Alexander von Beregshasy has been
hand crafting museum quality reproductions of the famous Crown Jewels
of England, Austria, France and Russia, for more than two decades.
The largest collection of tiaras and some that convert into necklaces.
Including Count Alexander's own designs, classic and timeless for
chokers, necklaces, earrings, bracelets, rings, cufflinks, cravat pins,
shoe buckles and lavish jewelled bodice ornaments that flatters the waist.
Jewels are triple-plated in palladium, a rare precious metal closely
resembling platinum, and set with Austrian Swarovski Crystals
or Russian Cubic Zirconia stones.
Each jewel is hand-made and signed by Count Alexander.

Exclusively available at his Palatial Jewel Boutique at:
13 The Mall Antiques Arcade
359 Upper Street, Camden Passage, Islington, London N1 0PD
Telephone: (020) 7354 0058
www.countalexander.com

Open:
Tuesday to Saturday 11am to 4.30pm
Jewels can be hired for Film & Television only.
Count Alexander is a Period Jewellery Stylist for Films and for Brides.

204

ZONE PRESCRIPTION CARD
AND THANK YOU

SELFRIDGES&Cº

Tel: 0207 247 3883
Email: absolutevintage@hotmail.com
Absolute Vintage. 15 Hanbury Street London E1 6QR

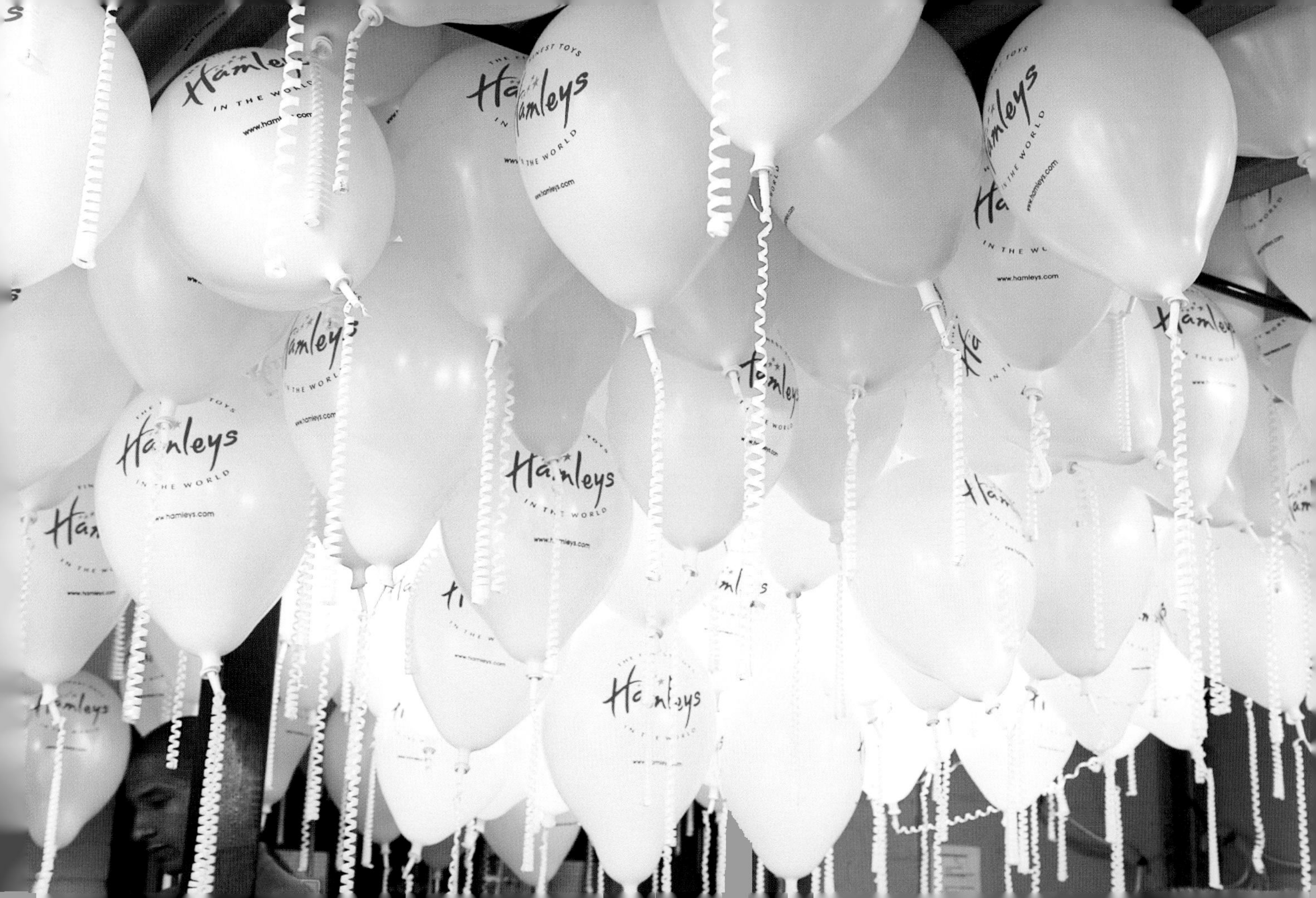
Hamleys
IN THE WORLD
www.hamleys.com

the directory

pp 16–17 Lords (builders merchants)
119–121 Westbourne Grove W2 4UP

pp 18–19 News-stand
55 Praed Street W2 1NR

pp 20–21 Lamborghini London (car dealership)
Melton Court, 27 Old Brompton Road SW7 3TD

pp 22–23 Brixton Meat Market (halal butcher)
28 Atlantic Road SW9 8JA

pp 24–25 Huntsman (men's outfitter)
11 Savile Row W1S 3PS

pp 26–27 Dragons (children's furniture)
23 Walton Street SW3 2HX

pp 28–29 A. Elfes Ltd (monumental stonemasons)
17 Osborn Street E1 6TD

pp 30–31 The Green Man (pub)
144 Essex Road N1 8LX

pp 32–33 Westland (antique fireplaces)
St Michael's Church, Leonard Street EC2A 4ER

pp 34–35 Zaco Mini Market (grocer)
175 Upper Street N1 1RG

pp 36–37 G. Smith and Sons (tobacconist)
74 Charing Cross Road WC2H 0BG

acknowledgments

Thank you to all the curators of these windows,
without whom this book would not exist.
Thank you to the team at Thames & Hudson in Paris
and to Sara Fenby in London.
Our sincere thanks also to Hattie Ellis.